THE ULTIMATE SPORTS PHOTOGRAPHY BOOK

Sports Illustrated KIDS

THE AMAZING WORLD OF
SPORTS

THE ULTIMATE SPORTS PHOTOGRAPHY BOOK

SPORTS ILLUSTRATED KIDS

Managing Editor	Bob Der
Creative Director	Beth Power Bugler
Photo Editor	Marguerite Schropp Lucarelli

Produced by
SHORELINE PUBLISHING GROUP LLC
Santa Barbara, California

President/Editorial Director	James Buckley, Jr.
Designer	Tom Carling, carlingdesign.com
Photo Researcher	Jackie Jeske

Text for this book was written by James Buckley, Jr., along with
David Fischer (Summer) and Ellen Labrecque (Winter).

Thanks to Karen Carpenter and the SI Picture Sales Department for their assistance.

TIME INC. HOME ENTERTAINMENT

Publisher	Richard Fraiman
Executive Director, Marketing Services	Carol Pittard
Director, Retail & Special Sales	Tom Mifsud
Marketing Director, Branded Businesses	Swati Rao
Director, New Product Development	Peter Harper
Financial Director	Steven Sandonato
Assistant General Counsel	Dasha Smith Dwin
Prepress Manager	Emily Rabin
Book Production Manager	Jonathan Polsky
Associate Prepress Manager	Anne-Michelle Gallero
Associate Marketing Manager	Alexandra Bliss

Special thanks: Victoria Alfonso, Bozena Bannett, Glenn Buonocore, Suzanne Janso, Robert Marasco, Brooke McGuire, Chavaughn Raines, Ilene Schreider, Adriana Tierno, Britney Williams

ISBN: 1-933821-00-0

Time Inc. Home Entertainment is a trademark of Time Inc.

10 9 8 7 6 5 4 3 2 1 6 7 8 9 10

Printed in the United States.

Pages 2-3: Dustin Miller gets enormous air. PHOTOGRAPH BY BO BRIDGES

Page 5: Dirk Nowitzki of the Dallas Mavericks rises to the hoop. PHOTOGRAPH BY GREG NELSON

TABLE OF CONTENTS

INTRODUCTION
CAPTURING MEMORIES

This amazing book of sports photography would not have been possible without two kinds of stars. One kind is obvious—the awesome athletes whose actions, talent, and emotion are on display in big, beautiful pictures. The other kind of star doesn't appear in person, but without them, we'd have nothing but a big book of white pages. We're talking about sports photographers, of course.

Sports photographers combine a sharp eye, a knowledge of sports, and years of training to capture moments that will never happen again. Think about it: Sportswriters can take hours or days to carefully describe what they have seen. They can talk to people, look up stats, or watch the key moment again on video. A sports photographer has one chance to get a picture, a fraction of a second to snap the shutter and capture a moment forever. No pressure, right?

Before we start our tour of amazing sports pictures, let's hear a little bit from some of the people behind the lens, the other stars of this book, about the work they do.

One very cool thing about being a sports photographer is obvious: You get to watch a lot of sports. Even better is that part of your job is becoming an expert in sports, especially the ones that you plan to photograph.

"The more you watch sports and teams and the more you experience the sports, the better chance you'll have to get the shot you want," says SPORTS ILLUSTRATED staff photographer Bob Rosato. "You have to understand the game and the

John W. McDonough/Spots Illustrated

players. That lets you anticipate the action, and anticipation is the key to photographing sports. You have to see what's going to happen before it happens."

One good example is on page 168. For that photo of Hines Ward scoring in Super Bowl XL, SI staff photographer John McDonough had two cameras ready, just in case. Planning ahead, he had a long lens to take a photo of the action at the line, 45 yards away. As the long pass to Ward happened and the Pittsburgh wide receiver sped toward McDonough's position, the photographer switched to a shorter lens to capture Ward running toward him.

"You have to be ready all the time," adds the veteran "shooter." "You just don't stop shooting. And don't stop looking after the play is over; every sports moment might have another moment, a reaction, right after it."

Understanding the sports also helps photographers make sure they're in the right place at the right time. SI senior staff photographer Heinz Kluetmeier noted that he and dozens of others took photos of the leaping touchdown by USC running back Reggie Bush in a November 2005 game against UCLA. But he says Peter Read Miller (see page 102) got the best one. You can see two other angles of the same play on the opposite page. It's the same play, but every photographer captures it from a different angle, creating another way of seeing the scene.

"Shooting from the corners [of the end zone] is a great place at a football game," says Heinz. "But when I got there, [my fellow SI photographer] Peter Read Miller was already there. Since we were working together for the magazine, I moved to the middle of the field. When Bush leaped, Peter had the best angle."

Heinz also brings up a point about taking risks. "On that shot, Peter took a chance and held his camera very low. He took a chance and got something that no one else had. Sometimes taking a chance lets you find a unique shot. Of course, a little luck helps, too!"

McDonough agrees. For a photo he took during the 2004 NBA playoffs (opposite), he moved from his regular baseline position to a spot higher up in the stands. "I decided to elevate. I pre-composed [set up visually what he would be photographing] and I made sure I wasn't blocked by anything. Then when Derek Fisher [of the Lakers, uniform number 2 in photo] made his last-second shot, I caught it at the right moment from an angle I knew would work."

In games like these, a photographer might take more than 1,000 pictures to end up with just one that perfectly captures a moment. But making sure that the moment is among those 1,000 pictures is what makes these photographers the best at what they do.

Technology, in the form of digital cameras, has meant enormous changes in photography. Photographers now have many tools to choose from that they didn't have before. Being able to quickly view the photo you've just taken means photographers don't have to wait to get their film developed to see how they've done. (Photo slang: When photographers all suddenly look down at the back of their cameras to check their shot after a big play, it's called "chimping.") However, Kluetmeier warns young (and old) photographers not to let the technology get in the way of the work.

"All of the things a photographer needs are the same: beautiful lighting, great emotion, a key play, great action. You still have to think and anticipate, put yourself in the right place," he says. "It doesn't matter if it's taken on film or digital or toilet paper, the most important thing is the picture. What is the emotional reaction to the photo in the first second someone sees it? The technology doesn't matter; it matters that you see something that you can capture to share."

AP/Wide World

John W. McDonough/Sports Illustrated

For sports photographers, that is the key to the job: capturing memories. "Put together the excitement of the games and the ability to capture a memory for others, and you get a real adrenaline jolt," says Rosato. "You just can't replace that feeling."

"Being a part of these exciting moments is great," adds Kluetmeier, "but being able to capture that emotion and excitement, to share those emotions with others, that's my main goal."

So, who are the most amazing people in this *Amazing World of Sports*? Now that you know a little bit more about the people who took the pictures, and after you've looked those pictures over — you make the call. —*James Buckley Jr.*

SPRING

Spring has sprung—and so has Albert Pujols, as the baseball season and Pujols's powerful bat get into full swing. Spring is the season for Opening Day and March Madness, for putting away the skis and getting out the skateboards, for the NASCAR season to heat up and for some college sports to wind down. Celebration is in the air, as champions are crowned in men's and women's college basketball, which you'll see in this chapter. Every game is a celebration for baseball fans when their team wins. In this photo, Pujols celebrates after hitting a walk-off homer to give his St. Louis Cardinals a win over the visiting Cincinnati Reds. Speaking of red, the new Busch Stadium was a sea of it behind Albert; they had a lot to see, too, as this was Pujols's third homer of the day. That's worth springing out of your seat!

PHOTOGRAPH BY DILIP VISHWANAT/US PRESSWIRE

Manny Being Manny

Ball is just about to meet bat as Boston's Manny Ramirez unleashes his powerful swing in a game against the Angels. Ramirez's bat has met a lot of baseballs in his 14-year career. He has 40 or more homers in five seasons and topped 100 RBI every year but one from 1995 through 2005. Manny and fellow Red Sox slugger David Ortiz form one of the most powerful hitting pairs in recent baseball history.

PHOTOGRAPH BY ROBERT BECK/SPORTS ILLUSTRATED

Did You Know?

Manny began his career with the Cleveland Indians in 1993 and played with them through 1999. In 1995, he helped the Indians reach the World Series. In 1999, his 165 RBIs were the most in the American League since Jimmie Foxx had 175 in 1938.

Trivia Challenge

Manny Ramirez's 20 career grand slams are second-most in major league history. What famous Yankees slugger holds the all-time career record for grand slams?

ANSWER: Lou Gehrig hit 23 grand slams in his Hall of Fame career.

Trivia Challenge

The Heat is actually Shaquille O'Neal's third NBA team. Name the team he started with and with whom he won an NBA scoring title in 1995.

ANSWER: The Orlando Magic chose Shaq with the first overall pick in the 1992 NBA Draft.

Shaq Slam!

Shaquille O'Neal helped the Los Angeles Lakers win three NBA championships (2000–2002). "Shaq Daddy" became a legend in L.A., but he and the team parted ways in the summer of 2004. Traded to the Miami Heat, Shaq was soon an equally large presence in South Florida, continuing the style of play that had made him an 11-time NBA All-Star.

PHOTOGRAPH BY
LISA BLUMENFELD/GETTY IMAGES

Adam's Eve

Hair flopping, mouth open, and elbows and knees flapping, Adam Morrison was one of college basketball's top players in 2006. Unfortunately, the Gonzaga forward ended his season in tears as his team lost to UCLA in the regional semifinals of the NCAA basketball tournament.

PHOTOGRAPH BY DAVID E. KLUTHO/SPORTS ILLUSTRATED

Did You Know?
Adam has diabetes, a medical condition that affects levels of sugar in the blood. It is very rare to find pro or college athletes who play with this condition, which can be dangerous and which Adam must monitor constantly. He often speaks with young athletes who have diabetes to encourage them to learn to manage the disease and still play sports.

13

Blue Sky over Alabama

It's a beautiful May day at Talladega Superspeedway as Jeff Gordon (No. 24, bottom left) leads the field through Turn 4 during the 2006 Aaron's 499. Gordon went on to win the race, his second straight Aaron's 499 victory. Gordon remains one of the sport's best-known drivers; his four season titles are second only to Richard Petty and Dale Earnhardt, Sr., each of whom won seven.

PHOTOGRAPH BY ANDY LYONS/GETTY IMAGES

TURN 4

Fun in the Sun

Beach volleyball superstar Misty May-Trenor is silhouetted against the bright spring sun as she leaps to make a serve. Misty teams with Kerri Walsh to form one of sport's most dominating teams. Through the middle of 2004, the duo won 90 matches in a row and topped off their amazing streak with a gold medal at the 2004 Summer Olympics. In 2006, they became the first women's team with 50 career tournament championships. Misty had some hops in the indoor version of the sport, too, winning national high school player of the year and NCAA All-America honors, before grabbing her sunscreen and heading to the beach.

PHOTOGRAPH BY ALEXANDER HASSENSTEIN/
BONGARTS/GETTY IMAGES

Trivia Challenge

In beach volleyball, there are two players on each team. How many players are on the court for each team in a game of indoor volleyball?

Did You Know?

Beach volleyball indoors? That's right, several events on the Association of Volleyball Professionals (AVP) Tour are held indoors or at locations far from a beach. Hundreds of tons of sand are trucked in and spread onto parking lots or on arena floors. Who says you can't have a beach in the middle of Cincinnati?

Another Triumph for Tiger

Tiger Woods, wearing the red shirt he always puts on for the final round of a golf tournament, blasts out of a sand trap on the 13th hole at Augusta National in 2005. Woods went on to earn his fourth Masters championship, draining a 15-foot birdie putt on the first hole of a sudden-death playoff with Chris DeMarco. The victory gave Tiger nine wins in "majors," golf's four biggest tournaments. His tenth major title came later in 2005, when Tiger joined the great Jack Nicklaus as the only golfers to win the Masters and British Open tournaments four times.

PHOTOGRAPH BY AL TIELEMANS/SPORTS ILLUSTRATED

Did You Know?
Earl and Kultilda Woods didn't name their son Tiger at birth. Instead, they named him Eldrick. He got his famous nickname from an old Army buddy of his father's.

Trivia Challenge
Through May 2006, Tiger Woods has won 10 "major" titles. Can you name the four golf tournaments known as the majors?

ANSWER: The Masters, U.S. Open, PGA Championship, and British Open

Hitting a High Note

See the neck of that giant guitar outside the Hard Rock Casino in Las Vegas? See that tiny figure floating there above the vert ramp? That's skateboard big air legend Danny Way plunging down onto the ramp. It's April 6, 2006, and Danny has just jumped a world freefall record 28 feet off a platform attached to the top of the guitar. He's on his way to landing — safely — on the enormous 56-foot ramp specially built for this trick. Way to go, Way!

PHOTOGRAPH BY TODD BIGELOW/AURORA

BUILD RAMPS NOT BOMBS

Did You Know?

Danny is the creator of the MegaRamp, skateboarding's most outrageous venue. Danny has taken the MegaRamp to China (see page 72), Mexico, and all over the United States. The top of the MegaRamp can be as high as 70 feet above the ground. Skaters dropping into the MegaRamp roar down the side and can find themselves seconds later soaring over 60-foot gaps with nothing between them and the ground except their skateboard and skill.

Trivia Challenge

Danny's riding a skateboard with wheels made of polyurethane, a type of plastic. But that's not what skateboard wheels have always been made of. What earthy substance was used to make the first skateboard wheels?

ANSWER: Clay wheels were the standard until Frank Nasworthy invented urethane wheels in 1972.

21

Ohio's Red Sea

Too many people on the floor? Ohio State basketball fans stormed the court after their team's 2005 upset 65–64 win over No. 2–ranked Illinois. College hoops fans are among the most devoted — and loudest! — in sports, filling arenas with color and noise.

PHOTOGRAPH BY DAVID E. KLUTHO/
SPORTS ILLUSTRATED

Did You Know?

Most sports were developed over time, as many people contributed ideas to improve the games. Basketball, however, was invented by one man. Dr. James Naismith, a P.E. teacher in Massachusetts, wrote up the first 13 rules of basketball in 1891. The score of the first game was 1-0 (baskets were only one point at first).

Trivia Challenge?

What are the nicknames of these two Big 10 schools?

ANSWER: Illinois Illini; Ohio State Buckeyes

23

Did You Know?
The 2006 championship game marked only the second time that the national women's final that had gone to overtime. The first was in 1991, when Tennessee won the second of its record six NCAA women's titles in a 70–67 thriller over Virginia.

Trivia Challenge
What is the nickname of Maryland's athletic teams? And what does it mean?

ANSWER: Maryland's athletes are called Terrapins, which is the name of a type of turtle. The nickname is often shortened to "Terps."

Dancing at the Big Dance

For the Maryland women's basketball team, spring was a time to dance. They celebrated on the court in Boston after winning the 2006 NCAA championship. Maryland defeated Duke 78–75 in overtime after trailing by 13 points at one stage in the game. Though celebration is the theme of this photo, you can also see the opposite emotion; on the far right, you can see Duke's Abby Waner kneeling on the court holding her head, her championship dreams drifting away with the music.

PHOTOGRAPH BY BILL FRAKES/SPORTS ILLUSTRATED

Let the Confetti Fly!

The Florida Gator mascot leads the cheers as the confetti pours
from the ceiling at the end of the 2006 NCAA men's basketball
championship. Victorious Florida players are in a pileup at midcourt
as videographers and officials swarm around them, already preparing
for the postgame ceremonies. Amid the joy, though, look for the losing
UCLA team, in white, starting its long walk to the locker room.

PHOTOGRAPH BY JOHN W. MCDONOUGH/SPORTS ILLUSTRATED

Did You Know?

Immediately following most championship games, the players and staff are given T-shirts and baseball caps with their school's or team's name shown as the new champion. How are these items made so quickly? That's easy: Shirts and hats are made for both teams, but of course only the winners' gear is taken out of the boxes. The shirts showing the other "champion" are usually donated to overseas charities.

Trivia Challenge

Joakim Noah of Florida was named the tournament MVP. His dad has some experience holding up trophies, too. What sport did Noah's dad excel at?

ANSWER: Yannick Noah was the 1983 French Open champion.

27

Firing Away in Florida

Baseball teams greet the spring in Florida or Arizona as they gather to shake off the winter blues and get ready for the new season. During a 2006 game at the New York Mets' spring training complex in Florida, Pedro Martinez fires in a pitch. Veterans such as Martinez, assured of spots on the team, use the spring to tune up their games. Younger players, however, see spring training as a way to impress the team and perhaps earn a spot in "The Show."

PHOTOGRAPH BY TOM DIPACE

Daring Danica

Danica Patrick (number 16, bottom car) made history at the 2005 Indy 500 when she became the first woman to hold the lead of that famous race. She was in front of the field for 19 laps, including lap 193 of the 200-lap race. Though her car's fuel shortage caused her to fall to fourth place, she still recorded the best finish for a woman in the race's history. Her driving skills and positive personality made her one of the year's top sports stories.

PHOTOGRAPH BY SIMON BRUTY/SPORTS ILLUSTRATED

Did You Know?

The types of cars raced at the Indy 500 are actually named for the racetrack. Indy cars are open-wheel racers with an open driver cockpit, as opposed to the closed cockpit and covered wheels of NASCAR's stock cars. Indy cars take part in the Indy Racing League series held in North America.

Trivia Challenge

Who was the first woman to start in an Indy 500?

ANSWER: Janet Guthrie in 1977. She would go on to race in two more Indy 500s, with a best finish of ninth in 1978.

ANSWER: His real name is
Covelli Crisp, which his great-
grandmother shortened to
"Co." His siblings made it
"Coco." Combined with his
last name, he's a cereal-lover's
favorite player!

Papi Says, "Drink Your Milk!"

David "Big Papi" Ortiz welcomes Coco Crisp
to the Red Sox with a milk bath. Red Sox fans
are hoping that Coco Crisp does not turn soggy
in milk. Before the 2006 season, the speedy
outfielder was brought in to help replace Johnny
Damon.

PHOTOGRAPH BY GARY BOGDON

One Wet Winner

Putting a new spin on a tradition that has been part of the Indy 500 since 1936, 2005 winner Dan Wheldon dumps the racewinner's postgame drink on his head instead of his lips. The Indy 500, held since 1911 at the Indianapolis Motor Speedway, is one of the world's most famous races. Wheldon, a native of England, was the first person from his nation to win at Indy since Graham Hill in 1966.

PHOTOGRAPH BY JONATHAN FERREY/GETTY IMAGES

Let the Sun Shine!

Orioles pitcher Bruce Chen and the fans in the outfield bleachers enjoy bright sunshine during an April 2006 game at Baltimore's Camden Yards. The ballpark opened in 1992 as the first of the "new" ballparks that combined classic design with modern extras such as luxury boxes. The fans on this sunny Saturday could enjoy only the weather, however, as the hometown O's lost to the visiting Seattle Mariners 8–6.

PHOTOGRAPH BY MARK GOLDMAN/ICON SMI

Did You Know?
Most baseball fields are built facing north or south, so that the setting sun won't be in the batter's or pitcher's eyes. Of course, that means the sun might be in the outfielder's or first baseman's eyes, so that's why they wear sunglasses!

Trivia Challenge
In 1970, a quartet of Baltimore pitchers did something that no other pitching staff has done. What was it and how many of the pitchers can you name?

ANSWER: Four Orioles pitchers each won 20 games or more: Dave McNally won 21 games, and Jim Palmer, Mike Cuellar, and Pat Dobson each won 20.

A Hair-raising Sport

Rugby is played around the world; its combination of speed and crunching tackles (no pads!) attracts huge crowds in many countries, though it hasn't quite caught on in the United States. This photograph was taken during a European tournament called the Six Nations. Italy's Paul Griffen has a solid hold on the jersey of France's Thomas Lievremont. Why all the tape on Griffen's head? He suffered a cut on his forehead earlier in the game. He went to the sidelines, got bandaged up, and went back into the action. Did we mention how tough you have to be to play rugby?

PHOTOGRAPH BY DAMIEN MEYER/AFP/GETTY IMAGES

Bryant Beats the Buzzer

Every eye is on the ball as Kobe Bryant lets a shot go with 0.9 seconds in this 2006 NBA playoff game. Less than a second later, the ball went in the hoop, setting off a celebration at the Staples Arena as the Lakers beat the Suns 99–98. While the subjects of the photo are all focused on the ball, photographer John McDonough had to focus on the entire scene. With one chance to get the shot, he had to wait for the right split-second to take this photo. Like Kobe, he nailed it.

PHOTOGRAPH BY JOHN W. MCDONOUGH/SPORTS ILLUSTRATED

Here's the Windup, Aaand . . .

. . . the pitch! Michigan pitcher Jennie Ritter is just about to whip her arm forward and deliver a pitch in a softball game against Washington in May 2005. Softball pitchers can top 70 miles per hour with their pitches, and that's from a mound 45 feet from home plate. Talented pitchers such as Ritter can make the ball rise, curve, or drop with amazing accuracy. You won't see a lot of slugfests in top-level women's softball.

PHOTOGRAPH BY JOHN BIEVER/
SPORTS ILLUSTRATED

Corey and The Beanstalk

At most ballparks, outfielders leaping to make spectacular catches at outfield walls can depend on padding to take away the sting. Not so at Wrigley Field, which has nothing but a covering of ivy vines on its hard brick walls. The chance of a bruise or a bump didn't stop the Cubs' Corey Patterson, however, as he made like Jack and leaped up the ivy to haul in this catch in a 2005 game against the crosstown rival White Sox.

PHOTOGRAPH BY JOHN BIEVER/ SPORTS ILLUSTRATED

Did You Know?
The famous ivy that covers Wrigley's brick walls was first planted in 1937. The first plants were actually small trees, but the winds in Chicago tore off all the leaves. The stronger ivy plants prospered and soon added green charm to one of baseball's trademark ballparks.

41

Did You Know?

David Ortiz was the 2005 designated hitter of the year. Baseball was around for more than a century before the DH came along, however. It was not introduced – to the American League only, of course – until 1973. The first DH was the Yankees' Ron Blomberg, on April 6, 1973.

Trivia Challenge

What is the famous leftfield wall at Fenway Park called?

ANSWER: The Green Monster

Boston Thunder

That booming sound heard around Boston's Fenway Park often comes from the potent bat of designated hitter David Ortiz. But during this 2004 game against the Phillies, the source of the rumble was this rare head-first slide by the supersized slugger.

PHOTOGRAPH BY HEINZ KLUETMEIER/SPORTS ILLUSTRATED

Up, Up, and Away!

That's where University of North Carolina's Marija Kurtovic aims to send the discus during the 2006 Texas Relays in Austin, Texas. Discus throwers spin quickly around in a small circle to gain momentum and power before releasing the metal discus. They try to throw it as far as they can to land within a triangular area. Marija's throw of 166´ 2˝ was good enough for seventh place.

PHOTOGRAPH BY KIRBY LEE/WIRE IMAGE

Did You Know?
The discus is one of the oldest events in track and field. It originated in the ancient Greek Olympics. Several famous statues of discus throwers demonstrate the classic form very much like that used today.

Trivia Challenge
Along with the discus,
can you name some
other objects that
are thrown (or "put,"
hint, hint) during field
events?

ANSWER: The spear-like javelin,
the heavy round shot put, and
the hammer, which
is basically a shot put on the
end of a three-foot wire.

Busch Pilot

Tony Stewart seems to be taking a new inside line during this April 2006 Busch Series race at Talladega, as his No. 33 Chevrolet Monte Carlo gets airborne. But stock cars make very poor airplanes, and Stewart's car was heavily damaged in the flipping, twisting landing. Stewart himself, though he didn't finish the race, was unhurt thanks to the many pieces of safety gear installed in his car.

PHOTOGRAPH BY SAM SHARPE

Did You Know?

Tony Stewart in a Busch series race? Doesn't he run in NASCAR Nextel Cup? Well, yes, he does, but several top Nextel Cup drivers also get rides in the Saturday Busch races, which use slightly less powerful cars and are usually a bit shorter in length. In fact, the all-time leader in Busch Series wins is Nextel Cup veteran Mark Martin, with 47, through May 2006.

Trivia Challenge

What is the name of the racing technique in which a driver follows another car very, very closely in order to cut wind resistance?

ANSWER: Drafting

All Eyes on Alou

Who will catch this foul ball — a fan at AT&T Park in San Francisco or Giants outfielder Moises Alou, racing toward the wall with glove outstretched? Moises ended up snagging this one, but the fans remain hopeful they'll get their own chance at catching a foul ball . . . and picking up a memorable souvenir.

PHOTOGRAPH BY BRAD MANGIN

Did You Know?
Moises Alou Is part of one of baseball's most well-known families. His father, Felipe, now the manager of the Giants, was a star outfielder himself in the 1960s. Felipe's brothers, Matty and Jesus, also were big-league outfielders. In 1963, the trio filled the outfield for the Giants for one game, a major league first.

Trivia Challenge
On average, how many pitches does a baseball last during a major league game before it is replaced or taken out of play?

ANSWER: Six pitches

In the Nick of Time

First baseman Nick Johnson of the Washington Nationals reaches for the throw just a flash ahead of the arrival of baserunner Austin Kearns of the Cincinnati Reds. Photographer Simon Bruty captured the action perfectly from his perch along the third base line, shooting across the diamond. The timing of the photo shows just how close many plays at first base really are; think how many more hits there would be if the bases were 88 feet apart!

PHOTOGRAPH BY SIMON BRUTY/SPORTS ILLUSTRATED

Did You Know?
The Cincinnati Reds are baseball's oldest pro team. They began play in 1869 as the Cincinnati Red Stockings, the first team made up solely of professionals. All other teams before that were officially amateur; that is, the players were not paid to play.

Trivia Challenge
The Nationals moved to Washington, D.C., before the 2005 season. Where were they located before that and what where they called?

ANSWER: Montreal, Quebec, Canada. They were called the Expos.

Did You Know?

A little inside stuff about umpires' gear: There's a good look at this home plate umpire's shoe. Looks pretty big, doesn't it? That's because he's wearing special shoes with heavy metal inserts to protect his feet against foul tips. Home plate umps also wear shin guards and chest protectors, plus, of course, a mask much like the catcher's.

Trivia Challenge

The Padres moved into a new ballpark in 2005. What is the name of their new home?

ANSWER: Petco Park

The Flying Padre?

Brian Giles of the Padres does his best long jump, but it wasn't enough as Marlins catcher Matt Treanor's diving tag clipped Giles on the foot before the flying Padre could land on home plate in this 2005 game at San Diego.

SUMMER

Wherever you spend it, summer is the season for getting outdoors and having fun. Surfer Jon Roseman cuts into the curl on this tasty wave on the South Pacific island of Tavarua (followed closely by photographer Warren Bolster), taking part in one popular coastal summer sport. And as schools empty out for the warmer months, it's time to hit the beach, the playground, the lakeshore, or just the backyard. For the pros, it's the heart of baseball season, and it's playoff time for the NBA and NHL. Every four years, of course, summer is the season for the Summer Olympics, for runners, swimmers, and more. Throw in some tennis, some NASCAR, and even a soap-box derby, and you've got one action-packed part of the year. See you at the beach!

PHOTOGRAPH BY WARREN BOLSTER

Second Base in Summer

Split-second timing is the theme of this picture, both for the action on the field and for photographer John Iacono's ability to freeze that action. During a Mets-Marlins game in July 2005, New York's Jose Reyes waits for both the ball and Florida's Alex Gonzalez to join him at second base. Gonzalez's timing was a little off on this steal attempt. He was out.

PHOTOGRAPH BY JOHN IACONO/SPORTS ILLUSTRATED

Did You Know?

In the major leagues, the time it takes for a baseball to go from pitcher to catcher to second base is about 3.2 seconds. The time it takes a good runner to get from first to second on a steal attempt is about the same. That's why most steal attempts are what the pros call "bang-bang" plays; both ball and player "bang" into the base at just about the same time. By the way, the time John Iacono used to capture this part of the action? 1/64th of a second.

Trivia Challenge

You can just see the umpire coming into the picture on the left. How many umpires are supposed to work each major league game? Bonus question: How many work in postseason games?

ANSWER: Regular-season games use a home plate umpire and one umpire per base, for a total of four "men in blue." Playoff games add umps down each foul line, making a total crew of six.

57

Did You Know?
Danny got his skateboarding career started early. When he was 11, he won the first competition he ever entered. He turned pro at age 14. By age 17, he was *Thrasher* magazine's skater of the year (1991).

Ramp to Ramp

The master of big air, Danny Way, shows that there is more than one way to make like a bird. He's in the middle of a huge leap from the ramp on the left to the one on the right. It's out of the frame, but the ramp on the left starts with a long downward slope. Danny rocketed down it, up the other side, and off the edge. He's aiming for a smooth landing on the longer run-out ramp on the right. We wish him luck. (P.S. He made it.)

PHOTOGRAPH BY MIKE BLABAC

Trivia Challenge
Who was the first skateboarder to perform a 900 – two and a half complete spins before landing again on a halfpipe?

ANSWER: Tony Hawk at the 1999 X Games.

Did You Know?

By winning the 2004 WNBA Finals two games to one over the Connecticut Sun, the Storm brought a national pro sports championship to Seattle for the first time since the Seattle SuperSonics won the NBA title in 1979. The win also made Anne Donovan the first female WNBA head coach to capture the title.

Trivia Challenge

Sue Bird is one of six women to win an NCAA championship, an Olympic gold medal, and a WNBA championship. Who are the other five?

ANSWER: Ruth Riley, Sheryl Swoopes, Swin Cash, Rebecca Lobo, and Kara Wolters.

Is It a Plane?

No, it's Sue Bird, the All-Star point guard of the Seattle Storm. Bird is flying towards the basket past Chamique Holdsclaw (1) for a layup against the Los Angeles Sparks at Key Arena in Seattle during the 2005 WNBA season. A year earlier, Bird overcame a broken nose in the playoffs to help the Storm win its first WNBA championship.

PHOTOGRAPH BY ROBERT BECK/SPORTS ILLUSTRATED

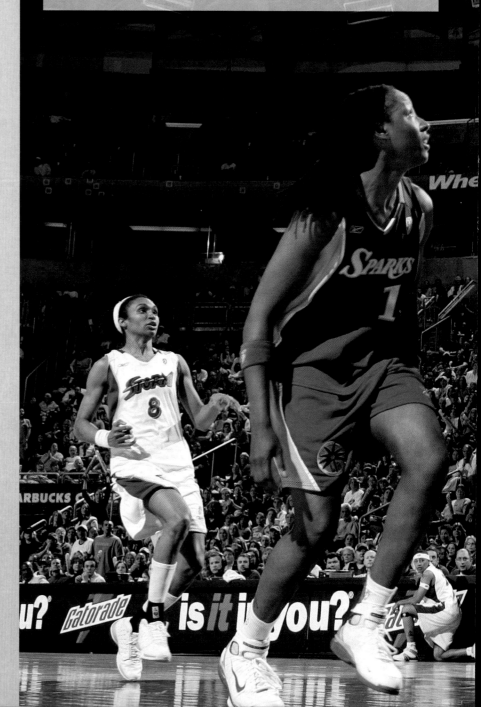

Rising to the Occasion

Roger Federer (near court) and Andre Agassi rally atop the world's highest tennis court. The two played on the 692-foot high converted helipad of the Burj Al Arab hotel (the world's tallest hotel!) in Dubai, United Arab Emirates, to publicize their semifinal match in the Dubai Open, in February 2005. Once on lower ground, Federer defeated Agassi in straight sets and went on to win the tournament for a second straight year.

PHOTOGRAPH BY DAVID CANNON/GETTY IMAGES

Did You Know?
Roger Federer has been ranked number 1 on the men's pro tennis tour every week since February 2, 2004. That's the third-longest consecutive-weeks streak at number 1 behind Jimmy Connors (160 straight weeks) and Ivan Lendl (157).

Trivia Challenge
In 2004, Roger Federer won the Australian Open, Wimbledon, and the U.S. Open titles. What was the Grand Slam tournament that he didn't win that year?

ANSWER: French Open

Eat My Donut Dust!

Greg Biffle smokes his tires after winning a NASCAR Nextel Cup Series race at Dover International Speedway in Dover, Delaware, on June 5, 2005. Biffle won six times in 2005. He finished second in the standings to Tony Stewart by just 35 points. This smoky celebration has become a tradition among NASCAR drivers.

PHOTOGRAPH BY EZRA SHAW/GETTY IMAGES

As Easy as Riding a Bike

Talented and high-scoring Arsenal forward Thierry Henry, in red, shows off his creativity by attempting this bicycle kick. The bicycle, or scissors, kick is one of soccer's most spectacular and daring plays. A player kicks up with one leg, then whips the opposite leg up after it, connecting with the ball (hopefully!) when the ball is above the player's head. If all goes well, the ball rockets toward its target. When it works, it's magical. When it doesn't, well, it's pretty embarrassing!

A Gymnast in Cleats

Playing goalie in soccer, some people say, is 85 minutes of boredom and 5 minutes of terror. A goalie might not see action for a long stretch of time, but they must be instantly ready to react to a shot. Tim Howard did just that when he made this spectacular diving save for Manchester United during a 2004 exhibition game in Philadelphia against the Spanish club Barcelona. Tim made headlines that year when the wildly popular United team signed him to be their first American goalie.

PHOTOGRAPH BY AL TIELMANS/
SPORTS ILLUSTRATED

Did You Know?

Thierry Henry also plays for the French national team. He helped them win the 1998 World Cup, which was held in France. Talk about a home-field advantage!

Trivia Challenge

What is the name of the league in England in which Manchester United plays?

ANSWER: The Premier League. English soccer has five divisions, with Premier at the top.

Which Way Is Up?

The high-flying sport of windsurfing combines the challenges of sailing with the acrobatics of surfing. Venezuela's Ricardo Campello demonstrates both with this wave-topping maneuver during a competition off the coast of Spain. Windsurfers can use waves as launching pads to "get air" so they can make moves like this.

PHOTOGRAPH BY SAMUEL ARANDA/AFP/GETTY IMAGES

In Your Face!

Tim Duncan of San Antonio
Spurs has the upper hand
against Ben Wallace and the
Detroit Pistons. Tim scored
a game-high 25 points in
the Spurs' 81-74 triumph in
Game 7 of the 2005 NBA
Finals. The win gave the
Spurs their third title in
seven years.

PHOTOGRAPH BY JOHN BIEVER/
SPORTS ILLUSTRATED

Soft Landing

Sploof! That's sort of the sound that long jumper Dwight Phillips probably made when he landed in the sand pit after this jump. Dwight was competing in the 2005 U.S. Outdoor Track & Field Championships in California. Long jumpers sprint down a long runway before leaping off on foot from a takeoff spot. After their short flight, they need a soft place to land—and that's sand.

PHOTOGRAPH BY DARYL DENNIS/ICON SMI

Did You Know?

Tim Duncan, who was born in St. Croix, was one of the U.S. Virgin Island's top swimmers in his age group as a middle schooler. When he was 13, a hurricane destroyed his local pool. That's when Duncan gave up swimming to play basketball.

Trivia Challenge

Tim Duncan was the NBA Finals MVP in 1999, 2003, and 2005. He is one of four players to win the award three or more times. Who are the other three players?

ANSWER: Michael Jordan (six times), Magic Johnson (three), and Shaquille O'Neal (three).

Great Leap Forward

Skateboarder Danny Way looks like a fly on the wall — the Great Wall of China, that is! In July 2005, Way became the first person to successfully leap over the Great Wall without being propelled by a motor. Dropping in from a 65-foot-high mega-ramp, Way landed five jumps across the 70-foot gap at the Wall's Ju Yong Guan Gate, including three backside 360s. "My heart was pumping in my chest the whole time," says Way. "But I managed to pull it off."

PHOTOGRAPH BY MIKE BLABAC

Did You Know?
Lyn-Z Adams Hawkins, age 16, is the most daring female skateboarder thrashing today. At age 14, she won the gold medal in women's Vert at the 2004 Summer X Games by becoming the first woman to land a kickflip indy. She won silver in the same event in 2005.

Trivia Challenge
Who holds the record for most medals won in skateboarding at the Summer X Games?

ANSWER: Tony Hawk. The legendary skateboarder has won 15 medals – five more than than his closest competitor.

White and Red All Over

Argentina's Mariano Puerta dives on the red clay of Roland Garros Stadium in Paris, France, during his French Open quarterfinal match victory over countryman Guillermo Canas, on June 1, 2005. Puerta then beat Nicolay Davydenko in the semifinal, but couldn't muster enough magic against Rafael Nadal in the final.

PHOTOGRAPH BY BOB MARTIN/SPORTS ILLUSTRATED

Did You Know?

The French Open is the only Grand Slam tennis tournament played on clay. Wimbledon is played on grass, while the U.S. and Australian Opens are played on hard courts. Clay courts are soft, and play is slower than on grass and hard courts. When a ball is hit onto clay, it slows down and bounces higher than it does on other surfaces.

Trivia Challenge
When keeping score of a baseball game, what position number is always assigned to the catcher?

ANSWER: 2

WHAM!

The mask pops off the head of Chicago Cubs catcher Michael Barrett (8), but he holds onto the ball during a home plate collision with Brent Mayne (a fellow catcher, no less) of the Los Angeles Dodgers. The Dodgers won, 8-1, at Wrigley Field in Chicago on August 13, 2004.

PHOTOGRAPH BY TOM DIPACE

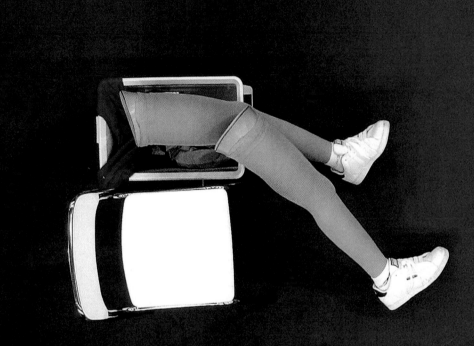

Stroke of Inspiration

With his prosthetics placed in the athlete's garment basket, Xavier Torres of Spain dives into the pool at the start of the men's 200-meter freestyle swimming heats at the 2004 Paralympic Summer Games, in Athens, Greece. Torres finished second in the heat, and fourth in the final. This shot was named the 2004 World Press Photo of the Year in the Sports Action category.

PHOTOGRAPH BY BOB MARTIN/SPORTS ILLUSTRATED

Sky Cycle

Why should skateboarders have all the fun? As halfpipes and vert ramps began to get popular at skateboarding events, freestyle BMX riders got into the action as well. Here, superstar Dave Mirra shows just how high a skilled rider can go. Because they can generate more speed, bikers can fly higher than skateboarders—but that means they have farther to fall, too!

PHOTOGRAPH BY MIKE BLABAC

Did You Know?

Dave Mirra came back from a terrible accident to reach the top of his sport. In 1993, he was hit by a car and badly injured. Though it took him several years to regain his strength, he came back to the sport he loved. He's still creating new tricks today.

Fish-eye View

Using a fish-eye lens while looking up from the bottom of an empty pool, photographer Mike O'Meally has created this wild scene. The sky is a blue circle above him, while on the left, skater Javier Mendizabel is doing a backside tailslide around the edge of the pool. Finding new and creative ways to take pictures is a big part of the sports photographer's life.

PHOTOGRAPH BY MIKE O'MEALLY

Yoooou're OUT!

Trying to execute a double steal, Guam's Trae Santos (16) is tagged out at home plate by catcher Matt Catonio as Canada completes a double play in Little League World Series action on August 21, 2005. Guam went on to win the game 5-0 at Lamade Stadium, in South Williamsport, Pennsylvania, but lost in the international semifinal to Curaçao.

PHOTOGRAPH BY GENE J. PUSKAR/AP

Did You Know?

The Maynard Midgets won the first National Little League Tournament (later the Little League World Series). They beat Lock Haven 16-7 in a battle of Pennyslvania teams in Williamsport, Pa. Founded in 1939 by Carl Stotz, Little League baseball has grown into an international organization. It is now played in more than 100 countries.

Trivia Challenge

Which current major league player helped Long Beach, California, win the Little League World Series title in 1992 and 1993, pitching two no-hitters in the '93 Series?

ANSWER: Sean Burroughs, now a third baseman with the Tampa Bay Devil Rays.

81

Flying Dutchwoman

Denise de Haan is holding on for dear life as she performs a move at the 2005 World Games wakeboard competition in Germany. Wakeboarders are pulled at the end of long ropes behind speedboats. (The speedboats create a wake, or set of small waves.) The athlete then performs jumps, twists, and spins over and around the wake.

PHOTOGRAPH BY LARS BAKKE/BONGARTS/GETTY IMAGES

Baseball Ballet

Yankees shortstop Derek Jeter shows off his hops while making a throw to first in a 2005 game against the Red Sox. Like most shortstops, Jeter uses his athletic skills to dive, jump, leap, or stretch to get any ball hit his way. Throwing while jumping isn't easy, but sometimes after a running stab, it's all you can do!

PHOTOGRAPH BY JOHN IACONO/
SPORTS ILLUSTRATED

Did You Know?

Derek Jeter wears uniform number 2. Yankees manager Joe Torre wears number 6. Those are the final two single-digit numbers not retired by the Yankees. Given the great success Jeter and Torre have had, they'll probably have their numbers retired someday, too. There's a good chance that no Yankee of the future will ever wear a uniform with a single digit.

Too Fast

Sprinter Allyson Felix was so fast during the women's 200-meter race at the 2005 World Track & Field Championships that not even a camera could catch her. She won gold at the event, part of a terrific year in which she was given the Jesse Owens Award as America's top female athlete.

PHOTOGRAPH BY ADRIAN DENIS/AFP/GETTY IMAGES

Trivia Challenge
The way Jeter's career is going, he's probably on his way to a spot in the Baseball Hall of Fame. Which of the following players is not a Hall of Fame shortstop? Honus Wagner, Johnny Bench, Pop Lloyd, Luke Appling.

ANSWER: Johnny Bench is a Hall of Famer, but he played catcher.

Pennant Stretch Dive

Rafael Furcal of the Atlanta Braves reaches second base before San Francisco's Ray Durham can apply the tag in the first inning of the Braves' 9-3 win over the Giants at Turner Field in Atlanta. Furcal had four hits and four RBIs in the August 2004 game to help propel Atlanta to its 14th straight division title. He now plays for the Dodgers.

PHOTOGRAPH BY CHUCK SOLOMON/SPORTS ILLUSTRATED

Surprise Return

During a smashing third set, Venus Williams ran down every ball — and eventually opponent Lindsay Davenport — to win her third Wimbledon singles title in 2005. Williams, who was seeded 14th, did not get past the quarterfinals of any Grand Slam event the year before.

PHOTOGRAPH BY SIMON BRUTY/SPORTS ILLUSTRATED

Did You Know?
The fuzz on tennis balls is actually a material called felt. The felt serves two purposes: It slows the ball down, making it easier to return a shot; and it allows the racket strings to grip the ball, helping players to hit with topspin or backspin.

Trivia Challenge
Which female tennis player won a record nine Wimbledon singles titles, including six in a row?

ANSWER: Martina Navratilova (1978-79, 1982-87, 1990)

Reflecting Pool

Photographer Heinz Kluetmeier captured Davis Tarwater — as well as the swimmer's reflection on the water's surface — in a 200-meter butterfly race at the 2005 World Championships in Montreal, Canada, last July. Tarwater missed the bronze medal by .26 seconds. Pawel Korzeniowski of Poland won the final.

PHOTOGRAPH BY HEINZ KLUETMEIER/SPORTS ILLUSTRATED

Trivia Challenge
What American swimmer won a pair of medals in the butterfly as part of his record seven gold medals in the 1972 Summer Olympics?

ANSWER: Mark Spitz, who set world records in all seven events he entered, including the 100- and 200-meter butterfly races.

Way . . .
Up in the Air

The King of Big Air, Danny Way, gets serious hang time while doing this grab high above the vert ramp. As the pictures on page 20 and 72 show, Danny's no stranger to acting like a bird on wheels.

PHOTOGRAPH BY MIKE BLABAC

Gravity Grand Prix

Matt Gravel (red cart) edges out Jimmy Fell as the two streak over the finish line during a rally of Soap Box Derby cars at a Cleveland track, on September 24, 2005. The margin of victory in most races is less than a tenth of a second, with winners moving on, and losers heading into an elimination heat.

PHOTOGRAPH BY KEITH SRAKOCIC/AP

Did You Know?

The All-American Soap Box Derby was founded in 1933 in Dayton, Ohio, by newspaper photographer Myron Scott. Then as now, the cars in the race are handmade and have no engines. They are raced by rolling downhill toward the finish line.

Trivia Challenge

Under what name do the Cub Scouts and Boy Scouts race small, handmade wooden cars?

ANSWER: Pinewood Derby

Hot Driver

Sparks from the car ahead of her showered Danica Patrick during the 2005 Bombardier Learjet 500 Indy Racing League race at the Texas Motor Speedway. Danica set off some sparks of her own, causing a media frenzy on her way to a 13th place finish. Tomas Scheckter won the race.

PHOTOGRAPH BY SIMON BRUTY/SPORTS ILLUSTRATED

Ready, Set, Splash

Like a pod of upside-down dolphins, this field of backstrokers arches off their starting spot. This race was held during the 2004 Summer Olympics. The backstroke is the only swimming race in which the competitors start in the water. They place their feet on the wall underwater and hold on to the pool rim with both hands. At the start, they leap backward and start stroking!

PHOTOGRAPH BY HEINZ KLUETMEIER/SPORTS ILLUSTRATED

Did You Know?
Freestyle BMX riding is a big part of the Summer X Games. Riders take part in street, flatland, and vert events, performing dozens of amazing daredevil feats of flying, balance, and acrobatics.

Trivia Challenge
Where does the name BMX come from?

ANSWER: The sport was first called "bicycle motocross." The X stands for "cross."

High Over the Humps

BMX freestyle rider Allan Cooke is upside down doing a one-footed-X-up backflip after zooming off the third of three humps of dirt. He's competing in a stunt dirt event in Denver. Riders use the series of small hills to get air and then do tricks while flying along in front of an amazed crowd of fans!

PHOTOGRAPH BY MARK LOSEY

One Monster Wave

The tiny figure at the base of this towering, moving mass of water is big-wave surfer Laird Hamilton. It takes a special kind of skill and bravery to plummet down the face of one of these monster waves, and Hamilton has been showing off that skill for years. Here, he's at Maverick, an enormous break off of Half Moon Bay just south of San Francisco, during the making of a movie on big-wave surfing. The waves at Maverick can reach 50 or 60 feet tall; an annual contest is held whenever the waves are going to be the highest. The waves are so big and fast that surfers have to be towed in behind Jet Skis rather than paddling in as with normal waves.

PHOTOGRAPH BY TONY FRIEDKIN/
SONY PICTURES CLASSICS/ZUMA/CORBIS

FALL

It's back-to-school time, but that's not what gets sports fans excited. It's back-to-football time! The NFL kicks off in September, and the first college football games are in late August. But it's in fall that the sport really rolls into high gear. The NFL is the most popular sport to watch on TV — that's 2005 NFL MVP Shaun Alexander (37) at the center of this pregame huddle with his fellow Seattle Seahawks. And millions of fans head to college campuses to see their favorite teams in action. Sports nuts don't just have football to watch, however, as both the NBA and NHL start their seasons in October. And baseball wraps up with the World Series, also known as the Fall Classic. In fact, fall would be the perfect sports season, if only there wasn't all that homework to deal with on weekends!

PHOTOGRAPH BY CORKY TREWIN

Trojan Horse

The final hurdle that separated Reggie Bush and USC from the 2005 BCS National Championship Game was crosstown rival UCLA in their annual showdown on December 3. Bush helped the Trojans clear it easily. He rushed for 260 yards and two touchdowns, including this 13-yard TD run, in USC's 66-19 victory. Bush's performance helped set up the championship showdown with number-two Texas in the Rose Bowl, which was won by the Longhorns.

PHOTOGRAPH BY PETER READ MILLER/SPORTS ILLUSTRATED

High-Flying Charger

LaDainian Tomlinson has become one of the NFL's top running backs — along with one of fantasy football's best picks — with a combination of speed, strength, and vision. Here, against the Philadelphia Eagles in 2005, he adds another weapon: flight! However, Eagles are pretty dangerous in the air themselves. They held L.T. to only 7 rushing yards in the game, which Philadelphia won 20–17.

PHOTOGRAPH BY SIMON BRUTY/SPORTS ILLUSTRATED

Did You Know?

L.T. has scored at least 10 touchdowns and rushed for at least 1,200 yards in each of his first five NFL seasons. He was drafted by the Chargers out of Texas Christian University with the fifth overall pick in 2001.

Trivia Challenge

L.T. was also the nickname of a Hall of Fame linebacker. Can you name this hard-hitting player and the team he played for?

ANSWER: Lawrence "L.T." Taylor played for the New York Giants from 1981 to 1993.

105

Score It Like Beckham

David Beckham, one of the most famous soccer players in the world, shows that he can celebrate as well as he can take his famous bending free kicks. He leaps into the arms of teammate Robinho after scoring a goal in Real Madrid's 4–1 win over Rosenborg, a team from Norway, in 2005.

PHOTOGRAPH BY MARCELLO RUBIO/ AFP/GETTY IMAGES

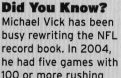

Did You Know?
Michael Vick has been busy rewriting the NFL record book. In 2004, he had five games with 100 or more rushing yards, an all-time best for a quarterback. His 119 rushing yards in a playoff game in 2005 were an NFL postseason best by a QB. And in a 2002 game against the Vikings, he set a single-game rushing record for quarterbacks with 173 yards on the ground.

Not Fuzzy, Just Fast!

A blur and a breeze: That's sometimes all that tacklers see and feel when going after the elusive Michael Vick. Photographer Scott Cunningham made this 2005 picture of the Atlanta Falcons' star QB out of focus on purpose. With the right sort of speedy subject and the eye of a great "shooter" (as photographers are sometimes called), a football photo can end up looking like a work of art.

PHOTOGRAPH BY SCOTT CUNNINGHAM/
GETTY IMAGES

Air Hockey

In an all-out effort to get to the puck, Serge Aubin of the Atlanta Thrashers sent New Jersey Devils forward Jamie Langenbrunner flying. Langenbrunner's about to land on the hard ice surface; good thing that he, like all hockey players, wears pads from head to toe. Hockey players know that falling down on the job is just part of the game.

PHOTOGRAPH BY JIM MCISAAC/GETTY IMAGES

Trivia Challenge
How many times have the New Jersey Devils won the Stanley Cup?

ANSWER: Three: 1995, 2000, and 2003

Did You Know?
The Atlanta Thrashers played their first season in 1999. They joined several other NHL teams in choosing bird nicknames (a thrasher is a type of bird often seen in Georgia). The Chicago Blackhawks and Columbus Blue Jackets (a type of jay) are the obvious birds. But don't forget the Pittsburgh Penguins! They might not fly, but penguins sure are birds.

Two Against 17

A pair of University of Miami defenders
lower the boom on Virginia Tech kick
returner Josh Morgan. Manhandling by
Miami was a theme in this big 2005 game.
Virginia Tech came into the game ranked
third in the nation, while Miami was ranked
fifth. The Hurricanes blew into Blacksburg,
Virginia, however, and won 23–7.

PHOTOGRAPH BY BOB ROSATO/
SPORTS ILLUSTRATED

Which Way Is Up?

L.J. Smith of the Eagles and Antonio Pierce of the Giants were probably very pleased they were wearing helmets on this play. After Smith made a catch, Pierce made the tackle, and both players ended up using their helmets for landing pads (they were uninjured on the play). At the end of the game, however, only the Giants were looking up at the scoreboard with joy; New York won 26–23.

PHOTOGRAPH BY NICK LAHAM/GETTY IMAGES

Trivia Challenge
A football rules question: If Smith had stayed on his feet, but put his hand down to regain his balance, would he have been ruled down?

ANSWER: No. An NFL player can put his hand down without ending the play. He is down when any other part of his body touches the ground after he has been contacted by an opponent.

Hot Corner Action

Once baseball gets to the postseason, players look for every little edge they can give their team. Chicago's Joe Crede went to great lengths to gobble up this grounder during the 2005 American League Division Series against the Boston Red Sox. White beat Red in this battle of the Sox, and Chicago went on to win the World Series.

PHOTOGRAPH BY DAMIAN STROHMEYER/
SPORTS ILLUSTRATED

Trivia Challenge
What was the slightly different original name of Chicago's American League team?

ANSWER: The team now known as the Chicago White Sox began play in 1901 as the Chicago White Stockings.

Passing Master

Steve Nash has turned the Phoenix Suns into one of the NBA's best and most exciting teams by combining creative, pinpoint passing with deadly-accurate outside shooting. In this play from February 2006, he doesn't mind that Boston's Raef LaFrentz is eight inches taller. Nash is going to take him on, whether to pass or shoot.

PHOTOGRAPH BY JOHN W. MCDONOUGH/SPORTS ILLUSTRATED

Fabulous Flying Football Player

University of Wisconsin defensive end Erasmus Jones didn't let a little thing like gravity stop him in his pursuit of Minnesota quarterback Bryan Cupito. Jones didn't stop Cupito from passing on this play, but his team did stop Minnesota. Wisconsin defeated its next-door neighbor, 38–14.

PHOTOGRAPH BY HEINZ KLUETMEIER/SPORTS ILLUSTRATED

117

MVP 1, Cy Young 0

Jermaine Dye of the White Sox got things off to a good start for Chicago in Game 1 of the 2005 World Series against Houston pitcher Roger Clemens. He's connecting here for what will be a home run to right field. The blast opened the scoring and helped the White Sox win the game 4–1. Dye ended up batting .438 in the World Series and was named the MVP. His hit in Game 4 drove in the only run of the night, as Chicago completed a surprising sweep to earn its first World Series title since 1917.

PHOTOGRAPH BY DAVID E. KLUTHO/ SPORTS ILLUSTRATED

Soaring Sox

Chicago second baseman Tadahito Iguchi
looks like he needs wings (and a soft landing)
during this play from the 2005 American
League Championship Series. Chone Figgins
of the Angels has just stolen second base, and
Iguchi's acrobatic stab of the throw from the
catcher prevented Figgins from moving on to
third. Middle infielders often need the skills of a
gymnast to field their positions.

PHOTOGRAPH BY CHUCK SOLOMON/SPORTS ILLUSTRATED

Manning in the Middle

Usually, Peyton Manning (18) is standing at
a comfortable distance from the action when
his Indianapolis Colts score. Often, he has just
tossed a pass that's been caught or carried into
the end zone (he set an NFL record with 49
TD passes in 2004). But in this AFC playoff
game against the Broncos in January 2005,
he took matters into his own hands, sneaking
across the goal line in a pile of players to score.
The touchdown gave the Colts a 35–3 lead,
and they went on to win 49–24.

PHOTOGRAPH BY SIMON BRUTY/SPORTS ILLUSTRATED

Did You Know?
Peyton Manning has only nine rushing touchdowns in his eight-year career (with a personal best of four scores in 2001). Steve Young holds the NFL career record for rushing scores by a quarterback, with 43.

Trivia Challenge
When Peyton Manning set the record for most touchdown passes in a season, whose record did he break?

ANSWER: Dan Marino of the Miami Dolphins threw 48 touchdown passes in 1984.

High Heat

You're sitting on the baseline at American Airlines Arena along with photographer Bob Rosato as the Heat's Dwyane Wade comes soaring in. You point your camera up, have a split-second to focus and frame the shot, and — *slam!* — click! Then you hope that Wade doesn't land on you. The exciting young guard helped lead the Heat into the 2006 NBA playoffs, thanks to athletic plays like this one.

PHOTOGRAPH BY BOB ROSATO/SPORTS ILLUSTRATED

Did You Know?

Longtime Los Angeles Lakers broadcaster Chick Hearn is credited with inventing the term "slam dunk" in the late 1960s, although basketball players had been dunking for years before that.

Trivia Challenge

What year did the Miami Heat begin play and what not-so-great record did they set in that first season?

ANSWER: The Heat's first season was 1988-1989. They set an NBA record by losing their first 17 games in a row!

Flying among the Jets

Sometimes the only way to gain yardage for your team is to take to the air. Tight end Randy McMichael was facing a trio of Jets during this 2005 game and became a new species of marine mammal: a flying Dolphin.

PHOTOGRAPH BY DAVID BERGMAN

Trivia Challenge
What feat did the 1972 Dolphins accomplish that has never been duplicated since?

ANSWER: They went undefeated for an entire season, going 17-0, including a 14-7 win over Washington in Super Bowl VII.

Block That Kick!

Perfect timing — twice! First, Anthony Reddick of Miami broke through at just the right moment to block this punt by Virginia Tech's Vinnie Burns. Second, photographer Heinz Kluetmeier snapped at the precise split-second to capture this big play. Reddick's timing and heroics weren't enough, however, as Virginia Tech won this 2004 game 16–10.

PHOTOGRAPH BY HEINZ KLUETMEIER/SPORTS ILLUSTRATED

Chicago Breaks It Open

Aaron Rowand was hitless in four at-bats, he got only two chances in the outfield, and he even broke his bat on this swing. It was a quiet night for Aaron, but a big night for the White Sox, who won Game 3 of the 2005 American League Championship Series. It was their second of four straight victories in the series after dropping the opener to the Los Angeles Angels. Chicago rode outstanding pitching and timely hitting to the A.L. and World Series titles in 2005.

PHOTOGRAPH BY JOHN W. MCDONOUGH/SPORTS ILLUSTRATED

Did You Know?
The first League Championship Series were played in 1969. Before then, the champions of the American and National leagues moved directly into the World Series. In 1995, baseball added another round of playoffs, creating a pair of Division Series for each league.

Trivia Challenge
Before they became the Los Angeles Angels of Anaheim in 2005, what were the Angels' three previous names?

ANSWER: They started as the Los Angeles Angels in 1961, became the California Angels in 1966, and were the Anaheim Angels from 1997 through 2004.

Jumping for Joy

White Sox catcher A.J Pierzynski leaps into the arms of closer Bobby Jenks to celebrate Chicago's 2005 World Series championship. The White Sox swept the Astros to win the first baseball title for the city of Chicago since 1917.

PHOTOGRAPH BY JOHN BIEVER/SPORTS ILLUSTRATED

Trivia Challenge
Now that the White Sox have won the Series, what major league team has gone the longest without capturing a world championship?

ANSWER: The Chicago Cubs, who have not won it all since 1908.

Did You Know?
Steve Smith led all NFL receivers with 1,563 receiving yards in 2005. He had come back after missing almost the entire 2004 season with a severe leg injury.

Soaring for Six

As he leaps toward the end zone, Steve Smith is probably glad that Will Allen of the Giants doesn't live up to his team's name. It would have taken a giant to haul in the high-flying Smith. Allen and his teammates didn't handle the rest of the Panthers any better, losing this 2005 NFC wild-card playoff game 23–0.

PHOTOGRAPH BY AL TIELEMANS/SPORTS ILLUSTRATED

Did You Know?

The New York Marathon is actually in the *Guinness Book of World Records*. The 2004 race holds the mark for most competitors in a marathon, with 37,257, of whom 36,562 finished the grueling run. The first New York Marathon in 1970 had only 55 finishers!

Trivia Challenge

What is the exact distance of a marathon?

ANSWER: 26 miles, 385 yards

Another Kind of Traffic Jam

Traffic was moving more smoothly than usual on the Verrazano-Narrows Bridge as runners in the 2005 New York Marathon thundered across it. The annual event sends tens of thousands of runners out into the city. The race course touches all five boroughs, or sections, of New York City, ending up in Central Park. Millions of people line the course to cheer the runners on.

PHOTOGRAPH BY MANNY MILLAN/SPORTS ILLUSTRATED

SPEED
LIMIT
45
RADAR
ENFORCED

Crowning a New King

LeBron "King" James has set the NBA on fire since leaping from high school to the pros in 2003. He has set several "youngest ever" records, including youngest player to score 50 points in a game (56 in a 2005 game), youngest player to reach 2,000 career points, and youngest player to start an All-Star Game (2005).

PHOTOGRAPH BY AL TIELEMANS/SPORTS ILLUSTRATED

One Up, One Down

At the 2006 NCAA wrestling championships, winner Troy Nickerson of Cornell University celebrates while loser Michael Sees of Bloomsburg holds his head in disbelief. This photo was taken from the ceiling of the arena by a remote-control camera.

PHOTOGRAPH BY GEORGE TIEDEMANN

Trivia Challenge

Iowa State wrestler Cael Sanderson made headlines in 2002 for something he *didn't* do in his four years in college. What did Cael not do?

ANSWER: Cael didn't lose a single match in his college career, finishing with an amazing 159-0 record. He was the only undefeated wrestler in college history.

Donovan Dances for Six

Donovan McNabb of the Eagles reaches out to cross the goal line in this 2004 game against Philadelphia's NFC East rival, the New York Giants. Part of the reason McNabb led the Eagles to the NFC Championship Game four times (2001–2004) was his running and scrambling ability. He has scored 21 rushing touchdowns in his seven-year pro career.

PHOTOGRAPH BY JULIE JACOBSON/AP-WIDE WORLD

Splashdown!

Logan Mankins of the New England Patriots doesn't let a little mud and water get in the way of his recovering a fumble during practice. Players such as Mankins, who only rarely sees action for New England, have to make every attempt to impress the coaches. Hustling play like this might mean a few more snaps in a game . . . along with a trip to the laundry!

PHOTOGRAPH BY BRIAN SNYDER/REUTERS

Let it snow, let it snow, let it snow! In the entire history of the National Football League, no regular-season game has been canceled by weather, so the Steelers and Bears were not going to let a bit of — okay, a lot of — snow get in the way of their 2005 game in Chicago. Tough weather conditions are part of a lot of winter sports, but they're also the reason some of those sports exist. The Winter Olympics would be pretty quiet without ice and snow, for instance. But not all the winter sports have to be played (or watched) while wearing mittens; winter is also a great time to watch sports indoors. Basketball and hockey seasons are in full swing, as fans look for their sports action in warm and toasty arenas. Of course, as the final picture in this chapter shows, just because it's cold and wintry here, it's sunny and hot in other places. Pull on your earmuffs and read on!

PHOTOGRAPH BY EZRA SHAW/GETTY IMAGES

Houdini of the Hardwood

Guard Kobe Bryant of the Los Angeles Lakers leaves Cleveland Cavaliers guard Sasha Pavlovic and center Zydrunas Ilgauskas wondering "Where did he go?" as he soars to the basket for a reverse layup. Bryant scored 23 points in this 94–88 Lakers victory on January 12, 2006.

PHOTOGRAPH BY JOHN W. MCDONOUGH/SPORTS ILLUSTRATED

Did You Know?

Though he was just 27 years old in the 2005–06 season, Kobe Bryant already ranked sixth on the Lakers' all-time scoring list. He trails only Basketball Hall of Famers Jerry West, Kareem Abdul-Jabbar, Elgin Baylor, Magic Johnson, and James Worthy.

Trivia Challenge

Kobe Bryant graduated from South Merion High School, in Philadelphia, and jumped straight in to the NBA. What team drafted Kobe and then traded him to the Los Angeles Lakers?

ANSWER: The Charlotte Hornets drafted Bryant with the 13th pick of the first round of the 1996 NBA draft. They traded him to the Lakers for center Vlade Divac.

Singing in the Rain

Quarterback Vince Young of the University of Texas Longhorns had plenty of reasons to celebrate as confetti poured from the sky. The Longhorns upset the University of Southern California 41–38 to win college football's national championship on January 4, 2006. Young passed for 267 yards and ran for 200 more yards, including an 8-yard touchdown run with 19 seconds left in the fourth quarter. He was named the Rose Bowl MVP for the second year in a row.

PHOTOGRAPH BY JOHN BIEVER/ SPORTS ILLUSTRATED

Trivia Challenge
Which team chose Vince Young in the 2006 NFL Draft? With which pick was he selected?

Did You Know?
Texas's 2006 national championship was its first outright title since 1969.

Gold in the Snow

Photographer Carl Yarbrough captured all the physical skills, snowy atmosphere, and intense focus of American skier Ted Ligety during the 2006 Winter Olympics. Ligety is shown here during one of the two runs of the slalom that were part of the men's combined event. Ligety took a commanding lead during the slalom, his specialty, and held on through the downhill portion of the event. His was the most surprising gold for the U.S. team in the Games, held in the snowy Italian Alps.

PHOTOGRAPH BY CARL YARBROUGH

Did You Know?
The first Winter Olympics were held in 1924, in Chamonix, France, although figure skating and ice hockey events had been held during some previous Summer Olympics. Norway won the most medals, with 17, in 1924. The sole gold medal for the United States was won by Charles Jewtraw in the 500-meter speedskating event.

Trivia Challenge
Can you name the five Alpine skiing sports held at the Winter Olympics?

ANSWER: Slalom, giant slalom, super giant slalom, downhill, and combined (two slalom runs plus a downhill run)

145

Blast Off

Four skiers cruise over a jump during the semi-finals of the Skier X competition at the Winter X Games in January, 2005. Skier X is a sport that combines motocross and downhill skiing. Racers compete at blinding-fast speed and race over tabletop jumps and banked turns.

PHOTOGRAPH BY BRIAN BAHR/GETTY IMAGES

Here's a Tip

The University of North Carolina tips off against its fiercest rival, Duke University, on February 7, 2006, as the players' shadows dance around them. The Blue Devils won the game 87–83, but the Tar Heels still hold the edge in the series, 124–96 (through 2006). The two schools are located just 11 miles apart, but rabid fans of each school feel like they come from different worlds.

PHOTOGRAPH BY BOB ROSATO/SPORTS ILLUSTRATED

Did You Know?
North Carolina has won four men's national basketball championships, while Duke has won three.

Trivia Challenge
Who did North Carolina beat to win the 2005 national title?

ANSWER: The Tar Heel defeated the University of Illinois 75–70.

149

Snowboarding was first called snurfing because it was like surfing on snow. Several people created early models of snowboards, but it was Jake Burton's fiberglass snowboard, invented in 1979, that helped the sport boom in popularity. Burton put bindings on top of light and easily maneuvered snowboards. Riders could easily take the skills of skateboards and surfing to the snow.

Click Until He Sticks

Pro snowboarder Jesse Fox sticks a backside 540 while photographer Scott Serfas captures the sequence with his digital camera. For this December 2005 photo, taken in Stewart, British Columbia, Canada, Serfas shot multiple photos. He then combined the pictures to show the trick in all its stages.

PHOTOGRAPH BY SCOTT SERFAS

151

Vin-sanity

Guard Vince Carter of the New Jersey Nets goes in for a tomahawk jam during a regular-season game against the Washington Wizards. Carter is known for his spectacular, high-flying dunks (he was nicknamed "Air Canada" when he played with the Toronto Raptors). Carter is a six-time NBA All-Star and has averaged 23.9 points during his nine-season career. He scored 19 points in this 89–83 win over Washington on November 19, 2005.

PHOTOGRAPH BY MANNY MILLAN/SPORTS ILLUSTRATED

Pucks-eye View

Photographer Bill Wippert got up close and puck personal at this 2006 NHL hockey game between the Ottawa Senators and the Buffalo Sabres. The spots on the photo are from ice melting on the camera lens. Photographers have to use quick shutter speed to capture NHL action: Skaters reach speeds of 20 miles per hour.

PHOTOGRAPH BY BILL WIPPERT

Did You Know?
The best NHL goalie named each season is awarded the Vezina Trophy. It is named for Georges Vezina, a goalie for the Montreal Canadians who died of tuberculosis in 1926.

Trivia Challenge
Name the NHL goalie who won the Vezina Trophy six times since the 1993-94 season.

ANSWER: Dominik Hasek won the trophy six times as a goalie for the Buffalo Sabres. He played for the Ottawa Senators in the 2005-06 season.

Skate the Line

U.S. short-track speedskater Apolo Anton Ohno (No. 254) zooms into first place during the semi-finals of the 1,500-meter race at the 2006 Winter Olympics in Turin, Italy. Ohno did not win a medal in this event, but he did capture gold in the 500 meters. He also won two bronzes in Torino (1,000 meters and 5,000-meter relay). At the 2002 Winter Olympics in Salt Lake City, Utah, Ohno won gold in the 1,500 meters and silver in the 1,000.

PHOTOGRAPH BY DAVID E. KLUTHO/SPORTS ILLUSTRATED

Did You Know?
Ohno is tied with U.S. long-track speedskater Eric Heiden for most career medals (5) won by a U.S. male Olympian in the Winter Games.

Trivia Challenge
Where will the 2010 Winter Olympics be held?

ANSWER: Vancouver, British Columbia, Canada

Spike in the Snow

Quarterback Tom Brady of the New England Patriots shows the ball (and the Colts) who's boss. He just scored a touchdown against Indianapolis during an AFC Divisional Playoff game on January 16, 2005. The Patriots easily won the game, 20–3, and went on to win their third Super Bowl in four years. They defeated the Philadelphia Eagles in Super Bowl XXXIX 24–21.

PHOTOGRAPH BY HARRY HOW/GETTY IMAGES

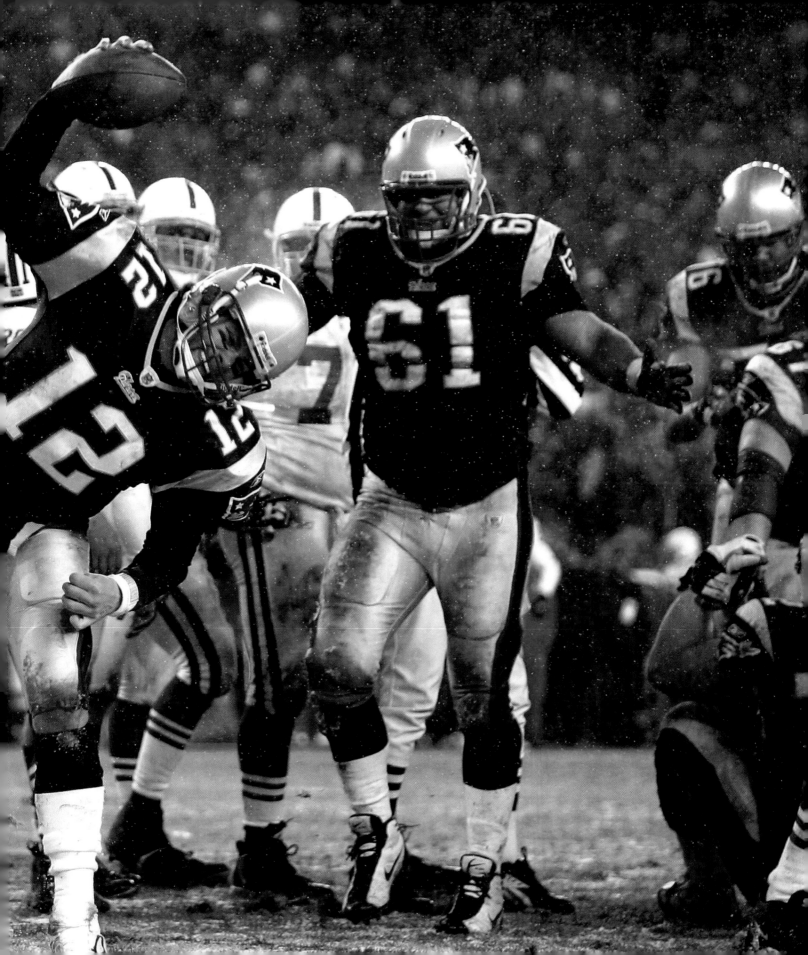

Little Man Nate

Rookie guard Nate Robinson of the New York Knicks soars to his first slam dunk contest championship at the 2006 NBA All-Star Game in Houston, Texas. Robinson may have the ups of a player who is seven feet tall, but he stands only 5'9" tall. "Everybody makes a big issue about height," Robinson says. "But as long as I play like a giant, it will be fine."

PHOTOGRAPH BY GREG NELSON

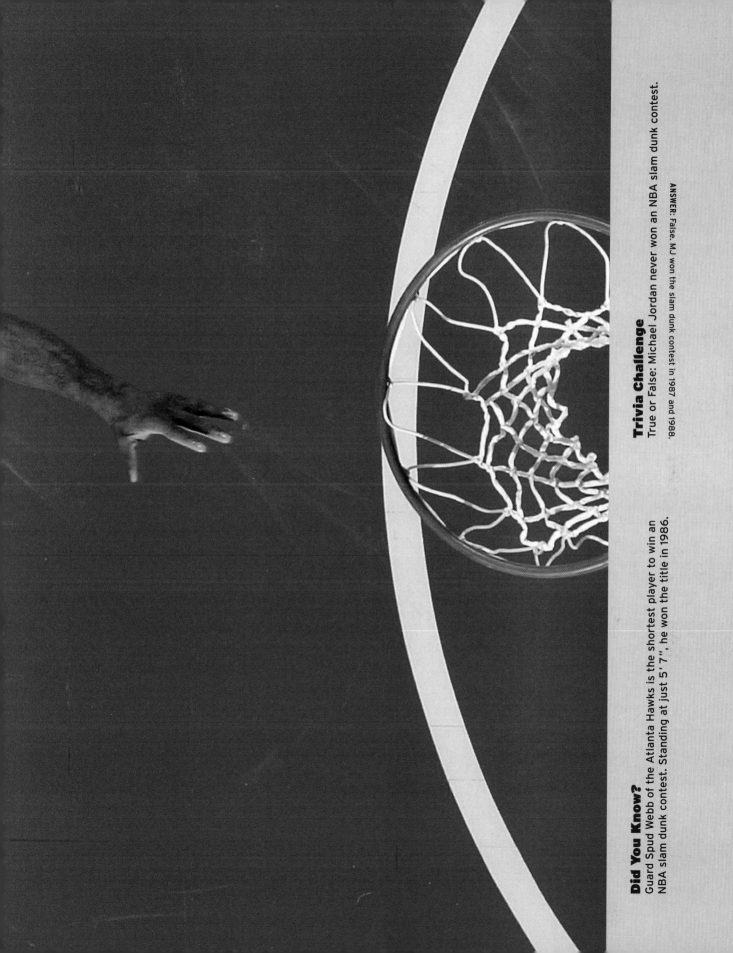

Did You Know?
Guard Spud Webb of the Atlanta Hawks is the shortest player to win an NBA slam dunk contest. Standing at just 5' 7", he won the title in 1986.

Trivia Challenge
True or False: Michael Jordan never won an NBA slam dunk contest.

ANSWER: False. MJ won the slam dunk contest in 1987 and 1988.

Rail Riding

Forget snowboard parks, pro boarder Seth Huot likes to take his tricks to the street. Here, he shows off by doing a frontside 270 on a handrail. Huot rides "regular," with his left foot in front of his right.

PHOTOGRAPH BY ANDY WRIGHT

A Vision of Grace

U.S. figure skater Kimmie Meissner appears ready for takeoff during her long program at the 2006 Winter Olympics. Meissner, who was just 16 years old at the Games, finished in sixth place overall. But just a month later, she won the gold medal at the World Figure Skating Championships in Calgary, Alberta, Canada.

PHOTOGRAPH BY HEINZ KLUETMEIER/
SPORTS ILLUSTRATED

Did You Know?
When Meissner won gold at the World Championships at age 16, she was one of the 10 youngest athletes in history to win the title.

Trivia Challenge
True or False: Meissner's Olympic teammate Sasha Cohen did not win a medal at the 2006 Games.

ANSWER: False. Cohen won the silver medal in Turin.

The Puck Stops Here

Defender Mark Giordano (46) of the Calgary Flames goes the extra inch to stop a puck from crossing the goal line in a fierce battle with the Vancouver Canucks. Despite Giodano's heroic efforts, the Flames lost in overtime 3–2, in this April 2006 game.

PHOTOGRAPH BY JEFF VINNICK/GETTY IMAGES

Did You Know?
To keep hockey pucks frozen and ready for play, officials keep a supply of pucks in a small refrigerator next to the ice. An official NHL puck is made of hard rubber, and is three inches across and one inch thick.

Trivia Challenge
How many NHL teams and how many NFL teams are located in Canada?

ANSWER: There are six Canadian NHL teams (Calgary Flames, Edmonton Oilers, Montreal Canadiens, Ottawa Senators, Toronto Maple Leafs, and Vancouver Canucks) and zero Canadian NFL teams.

TD or Not TD?

Quarterback Ben Roethlisberger of the Pittsburgh Steelers lies under several Seattle Seahawks as he looks to the officials to find out whether or not he had sneaked the ball into the end zone in Super Bowl XL. Roethlisberger threw for 125 yards and ran for 25 more in the game on February 5, 2006, and the Steelers won 21–10. Oh, the answer to the question: TD or not TD? *Touchdown!*

PHOTOGRAPH BY AL TIELEMANS/
SPORTS ILLUSTRATED

Ward Becomes a Winner

Hines Ward doesn't need words to express his excitement. His body language says it all. The wide receiver for the Pittsburgh Steelers celebrates a 43-yard touchdown catch against the Seattle Seahawks in Super Bowl XL. The Steelers won the game 21–10, and Ward was named the Super Bowl MVP. He caught five passes for 123 yards and one touchdown.

PHOTOGRAPH BY JOHN W. MCDONOUGH/SPORTS ILLUSTRATED

Pucker Up, Bus!

Running back Jerome "the Bus" Bettis plants one on the Super Bowl championship trophy after the Steelers won the 2006 game 21–10 over the Seattle Seahawks. The Bus, who played in the NFL for 13 seasons, retired after finally winning his first Super Bowl ring. One of the best big backs of his era, Bettis was called the Bus because of the way he ran over defenders.

PHOTOGRAPH BY AL TIELEMANS/SPORTS ILLUSTRATED

In Full Bloom

Golfer Michelle Wie looks as proud as a peacock as she drives from the fifth tee of the 2005 LPGA Samsung Championship in Palm Desert, California. A native of Hawaii, Michelle has golfed in winter, summer, fall, and spring her entire life. At just 16 years old, she was ranked second in the women's world golf rankings through April 2006. She had also pocketed about $10 million in endorsement deals.

PHOTOGRAPH BY REED SAXON/AP

Did You Know?
The Super Bowl championship trophy is named the Vince Lombardi Trophy after the legendary Green Bay Packers head coach. Lombardi coached the Packers from 1958 to 1968 and led them to six divisional titles and five NFL championships.

Trivia Challenge
Who won the LPGA Championship in 2003, 2004, and 2005?

ANSWER: Annika Sorenstam of Stockholm, Sweden, who is considered the best female golfer in the world.

Number 48 Is Number 1

Confetti is about the only thing that could slow down Jimmie Johnson. The 30-year-old driver stands in the drivers-side window opening as he celebrates his first Daytona 500 victory on February 19, 2006. Johnson has always had the need for speed. By the time he was eight years old, he was racing on motorcycles and winning championships.

PHOTOGRAPH BY JEFF VINNICK/GETTY IMAGES

Did You Know?
NASCAR drivers reach speeds exceeding 200 miles per hour.

Trivia Challenge
What does NASCAR stand for?

ANSWER: National Association for Stock Car Auto Racing

Did You Know?
The first Dakar Rally took place in 1979, and the competitors started from Paris, France.

Trivia Challenge
Where is Senegal located?

ANSWER: Senegal is located on the West coast of Africa.

Who Needs Camels?

Crossing the desert can be tough any way it's tackled, but riding on a motorcycle at least makes it more fun. These four riders are participating in a famous off-road endurance race called the Dakar Rally in December 2004. Competitors on various off-road vehicles cover several hundred miles a day and travel over dunes, mud, and deserts, in dangerous conditions. The starting place of the race changes each year, but the finish line is always in Dakar, Senegal.

PHOTOGRAPH BY DPPI/ICON SMI

INDEX